WELCOME TO OUR CABIN!

Dear visitor,

_____

_____

_____

Guest Names: _____

Dates Of Stay: _____ to _____

Traveling From: _____

Message To Host:

Favorite Lasting Memories From My Stay: _____

_____

_____

_____

Places I recommend To Others: (Restaurants, Shopping, Activities, etc...)

_____

_____

_____

Guest Names: _____

Dates Of Stay: _____ to _____

Traveling From: _____

Message To Host:

Favorite Lasting Memories From My Stay: _____

_____

_____

_____

Places I recommend To Others: (Restaurants, Shopping, Activities, etc...)

_____

_____

_____

Guest Names: _____

Dates Of Stay: _____ to _____

Traveling From: _____

Message To Host:

Favorite Lasting Memories From My Stay: _____

_____

_____

_____

Places I recommend To Others: (Restaurants, Shopping, Activities, etc...)

_____

_____

_____

Guest Names: _____

Dates Of Stay: _____ to _____

Traveling From: _____

Message To Host:

Favorite Lasting Memories From My Stay: _____

_____

_____

_____

Places I recommend To Others: (Restaurants, Shopping, Activities, etc...)

_____

_____

_____

Guest Names: _____

Dates Of Stay: _____ to _____

Traveling From: _____

Favorite Lasting Memories From My Stay: _____

_____

_____

_____

Places I recommend To Others: (Restaurants, Shopping, Activities, etc...)

_____

_____

_____

Message To Host:

Guest Names: _____

Dates Of Stay: _____ to _____

Traveling From: _____

Message To Host:

Favorite Lasting Memories From My Stay: _____

_____

_____

_____

Places I recommend To Others: (Restaurants, Shopping, Activities, etc...)

_____

_____

_____

Guest Names: _____

Dates Of Stay: _____ to _____

Traveling From: _____

Message To Host:

Favorite Lasting Memories From My Stay: _____

_____

_____

_____

Places I recommend To Others: (Restaurants, Shopping, Activities, etc...)

_____

_____

_____

Guest Names: _____

Dates Of Stay: _____ to _____

Traveling From: _____

Message To Host:

Favorite Lasting Memories From My Stay: _____

_____

_____

_____

Places I recommend To Others: (Restaurants, Shopping, Activities, etc...)

_____

_____

_____

Guest Names: _____

Dates Of Stay: _____ to _____

Traveling From: _____

Message To Host:

Favorite Lasting Memories From My Stay: _____

_____

_____

_____

Places I recommend To Others: (Restaurants, Shopping, Activities, etc...)

_____

_____

_____

Guest Names: _____

Dates Of Stay: _____ to _____

Traveling From: _____

Message To Host:

Favorite Lasting Memories From My Stay: _____

_____

_____

_____

Places I recommend To Others: (Restaurants, Shopping, Activities, etc...)

_____

_____

_____

Guest Names: _____

Dates Of Stay: _____ to _____

Traveling From: _____

Message To Host:

Favorite Lasting Memories From My Stay: _____

_____

_____

_____

Places I recommend To Others: (Restaurants, Shopping, Activities, etc...)

_____

_____

_____

Guest Names: _____

Dates Of Stay: _____ to _____

Traveling From: _____

Message To Host:

Favorite Lasting Memories From My Stay: _____

_____

_____

_____

Places I recommend To Others: (Restaurants, Shopping, Activities, etc...)

_____

_____

_____

Guest Names: _____

Dates Of Stay: _____ to _____

Traveling From: _____

Message To Host:

Favorite Lasting Memories From My Stay: _____

_____

_____

_____

Places I recommend To Others: (Restaurants, Shopping, Activities, etc...)

_____

_____

_____

Guest Names: _____

Dates Of Stay: _____ to _____

Traveling From: _____

Message To Host:

Favorite Lasting Memories From My Stay: _____

_____

_____

_____

Places I recommend To Others: (Restaurants, Shopping, Activities, etc...)

_____

_____

_____

Guest Names: _____

Dates Of Stay: _____ to _____

Traveling From: _____

Message To Host:

Favorite Lasting Memories From My Stay: _____

_____

_____

_____

Places I recommend To Others: (Restaurants, Shopping, Activities, etc...)

_____

_____

_____

Guest Names: _____

Dates Of Stay: _____ to _____

Traveling From: _____

Message To Host:

Favorite Lasting Memories From My Stay: _____

_____

_____

_____

Places I recommend To Others: (Restaurants, Shopping, Activities, etc...)

_____

_____

_____

Guest Names: _____

Message To Host:

Dates Of Stay: _____ to _____

Traveling From: _____

Favorite Lasting Memories From My Stay: _____

_____

_____

_____

Places I recommend To Others: (Restaurants, Shopping, Activities, etc...)

_____

_____

_____

Guest Names: _____

Dates Of Stay: _____ to _____

Traveling From: _____

Message To Host:

Favorite Lasting Memories From My Stay: _____

_____

_____

_____

Places I recommend To Others: (Restaurants, Shopping, Activities, etc...)

_____

_____

_____

Guest Names: _____

Dates Of Stay: _____ to _____

Traveling From: _____

Message To Host:

Favorite Lasting Memories From My Stay: _____

_____

_____

_____

Places I recommend To Others: (Restaurants, Shopping, Activities, etc...)

_____

_____

_____

Guest Names: _____

Dates Of Stay: _____ to _____

Traveling From: _____

Message To Host:

Favorite Lasting Memories From My Stay: _____

_____

_____

_____

Places I recommend To Others: (Restaurants, Shopping, Activities, etc...)

_____

_____

_____

Guest Names: _____

Dates Of Stay: _____ to _____

Traveling From: _____

Message To Host:

Favorite Lasting Memories From My Stay: _____

_____

_____

_____

Places I recommend To Others: (Restaurants, Shopping, Activities, etc...)

_____

_____

_____

Guest Names: _____

Dates Of Stay: _____ to _____

Traveling From: _____

Message To Host:

Favorite Lasting Memories From My Stay: _____

_____

_____

_____

Places I recommend To Others: (Restaurants, Shopping, Activities, etc...)

_____

_____

_____

Guest Names: _____

Dates Of Stay: _____ to _____

Traveling From: _____

Message To Host:

Favorite Lasting Memories From My Stay: _____

_____

_____

_____

Places I recommend To Others: (Restaurants, Shopping, Activities, etc...)

_____

_____

_____

Guest Names: _____

Dates Of Stay: _____ to _____

Traveling From: _____

Message To Host:

Favorite Lasting Memories From My Stay: _____

_____

_____

_____

Places I recommend To Others: (Restaurants, Shopping, Activities, etc...)

_____

_____

_____

Guest Names: _____

Dates Of Stay: _____ to _____

Traveling From: _____

Message To Host:

Favorite Lasting Memories From My Stay: _____

_____

_____

_____

Places I recommend To Others: (Restaurants, Shopping, Activities, etc...)

_____

_____

_____

Guest Names: _____

Dates Of Stay: _____ to _____

Traveling From: _____

Message To Host:

Favorite Lasting Memories From My Stay: _____

_____

_____

_____

Places I recommend To Others: (Restaurants, Shopping, Activities, etc...)

_____

_____

_____

Guest Names: _____

Dates Of Stay: _____ to _____

Traveling From: _____

Message To Host:

Favorite Lasting Memories From My Stay: _____

_____

_____

_____

Places I recommend To Others: (Restaurants, Shopping, Activities, etc...)

_____

_____

_____

Guest Names: _____

Dates Of Stay: _____ to _____

Traveling From: _____

Message To Host:

Favorite Lasting Memories From My Stay: _____

_____

_____

_____

Places I recommend To Others: (Restaurants, Shopping, Activities, etc...)

_____

_____

_____

Guest Names: _____

Dates Of Stay: _____ to _____

Traveling From: _____

Favorite Lasting Memories From My Stay: _____

_____

_____

_____

Places I recommend To Others: (Restaurants, Shopping, Activities, etc...)

_____

_____

_____

Message To Host:

Guest Names: _____

Dates Of Stay: _____ to _____

Traveling From: _____

Message To Host:

Favorite Lasting Memories From My Stay: _____

_____

_____

_____

Places I recommend To Others: (Restaurants, Shopping, Activities, etc...)

_____

_____

_____

Guest Names: _____

Dates Of Stay: _____ to _____

Traveling From: _____

Message To Host:

Favorite Lasting Memories From My Stay: _____

_____

_____

_____

Places I recommend To Others: (Restaurants, Shopping, Activities, etc...)

_____

_____

_____

Guest Names: _____

Dates Of Stay: _____ to _____

Traveling From: _____

Message To Host:

Favorite Lasting Memories From My Stay: _____

_____

_____

_____

Places I recommend To Others: (Restaurants, Shopping, Activities, etc...)

_____

_____

_____

Guest Names: _____

Dates Of Stay: _____ to _____

Traveling From: _____

Message To Host:

Favorite Lasting Memories From My Stay: _____

_____

_____

_____

Places I recommend To Others: (Restaurants, Shopping, Activities, etc...)

_____

_____

_____

Guest Names: _____

Dates Of Stay: _____ to _____

Traveling From: _____

Message To Host:

Favorite Lasting Memories From My Stay: _____

_____

_____

_____

Places I recommend To Others: (Restaurants, Shopping, Activities, etc...)

_____

_____

_____

Guest Names: _____

Dates Of Stay: _____ to _____

Traveling From: _____

Message To Host:

Favorite Lasting Memories From My Stay: _____

_____

_____

_____

Places I recommend To Others: (Restaurants, Shopping, Activities, etc...)

_____

_____

_____

Guest Names: _____

Dates Of Stay: _____ to _____

Traveling From: _____

Message To Host:

Favorite Lasting Memories From My Stay: _____

_____

_____

_____

Places I recommend To Others: (Restaurants, Shopping, Activities, etc...)

_____

_____

_____

Guest Names: _____

Dates Of Stay: _____ to _____

Traveling From: _____

Message To Host:

Favorite Lasting Memories From My Stay: _____

_____

_____

_____

Places I recommend To Others: (Restaurants, Shopping, Activities, etc...)

_____

_____

_____

Guest Names: _____

Dates Of Stay: _____ to _____

Traveling From: _____

Message To Host:

Favorite Lasting Memories From My Stay: _____

_____

_____

_____

Places I recommend To Others: (Restaurants, Shopping, Activities, etc...)

_____

_____

_____

Guest Names: _____

Dates Of Stay: _____ to _____

Traveling From: _____

Message To Host:

Favorite Lasting Memories From My Stay: _____

_____

_____

_____

Places I recommend To Others: (Restaurants, Shopping, Activities, etc...)

_____

_____

_____

Guest Names: _____

Dates Of Stay: _____ to _____

Traveling From: _____

Message To Host:

Favorite Lasting Memories From My Stay: _____

_____

_____

_____

Places I recommend To Others: (Restaurants, Shopping, Activities, etc...)

_____

_____

_____

Guest Names: _____

Dates Of Stay: _____ to _____

Traveling From: _____

Message To Host:

Favorite Lasting Memories From My Stay: _____

_____

_____

_____

Places I recommend To Others: (Restaurants, Shopping, Activities, etc...)

_____

_____

_____

Guest Names: _____

Dates Of Stay: _____ to _____

Traveling From: _____

Message To Host:

Favorite Lasting Memories From My Stay: _____

_____

_____

_____

Places I recommend To Others: (Restaurants, Shopping, Activities, etc...)

_____

_____

_____

Guest Names: _____

Dates Of Stay: _____ to _____

Traveling From: _____

Message To Host:

Favorite Lasting Memories From My Stay: _____

_____

_____

_____

Places I recommend To Others: (Restaurants, Shopping, Activities, etc...)

_____

_____

_____

Guest Names: _____

Dates Of Stay: _____ to _____

Traveling From: _____

Message To Host:

Favorite Lasting Memories From My Stay: _____

_____

_____

_____

Places I recommend To Others: (Restaurants, Shopping, Activities, etc...)

_____

_____

_____

Guest Names: _____

Dates Of Stay: _____ to _____

Traveling From: _____

Message To Host:

Favorite Lasting Memories From My Stay: _____

_____

_____

_____

Places I recommend To Others: (Restaurants, Shopping, Activities, etc...)

_____

_____

_____

Guest Names: _____

Dates Of Stay: _____ to _____

Traveling From: _____

Message To Host:

Favorite Lasting Memories From My Stay: _____

_____

_____

_____

Places I recommend To Others: (Restaurants, Shopping, Activities, etc...)

_____

_____

_____

Guest Names: _____

Dates Of Stay: _____ to _____

Traveling From: _____

Message To Host:

Favorite Lasting Memories From My Stay: _____

_____

_____

_____

Places I recommend To Others: (Restaurants, Shopping, Activities, etc...)

_____

_____

_____

Guest Names: _____

Dates Of Stay: _____ to _____

Traveling From: _____

Message To Host:

Favorite Lasting Memories From My Stay: _____

_____

_____

_____

Places I recommend To Others: (Restaurants, Shopping, Activities, etc...)

_____

_____

_____

Guest Names: _____

Dates Of Stay: _____ to _____

Traveling From: _____

Message To Host:

Favorite Lasting Memories From My Stay: _____

_____

_____

_____

Places I recommend To Others: (Restaurants, Shopping, Activities, etc...)

_____

_____

_____

Guest Names: _____

Dates Of Stay: _____ to _____

Traveling From: _____

Message To Host:

Favorite Lasting Memories From My Stay: _____

_____

_____

_____

Places I recommend To Others: (Restaurants, Shopping, Activities, etc...)

_____

_____

_____

Guest Names: _____

Dates Of Stay: _____ to _____

Traveling From: _____

Message To Host:

Favorite Lasting Memories From My Stay: _____

_____

_____

_____

Places I recommend To Others: (Restaurants, Shopping, Activities, etc...)

_____

_____

_____

Guest Names: _____

Dates Of Stay: _____ to _____

Traveling From: _____

Message To Host:

Favorite Lasting Memories From My Stay: _____

_____

_____

_____

Places I recommend To Others: (Restaurants, Shopping, Activities, etc...)

_____

_____

_____

Guest Names: _____

Dates Of Stay: _____ to _____

Traveling From: _____

Message To Host:

Favorite Lasting Memories From My Stay: _____

_____

_____

_____

Places I recommend To Others: (Restaurants, Shopping, Activities, etc...)

_____

_____

_____

Guest Names: _____

Dates Of Stay: _____ to _____

Traveling From: _____

Message To Host:

Favorite Lasting Memories From My Stay: _____

_____

_____

_____

Places I recommend To Others: (Restaurants, Shopping, Activities, etc...)

_____

_____

_____

Guest Names: _____

Dates Of Stay: _____ to _____

Traveling From: _____

Message To Host:

Favorite Lasting Memories From My Stay: _____

_____

_____

_____

Places I recommend To Others: (Restaurants, Shopping, Activities, etc...)

_____

_____

_____

Guest Names: _____

Dates Of Stay: _____ to _____

Traveling From: _____

Message To Host:

Favorite Lasting Memories From My Stay: _____

_____

_____

_____

Places I recommend To Others: (Restaurants, Shopping, Activities, etc...)

_____

_____

_____

Guest Names: _____

Dates Of Stay: _____ to _____

Traveling From: _____

Message To Host:

Favorite Lasting Memories From My Stay: _____

_____

_____

_____

Places I recommend To Others: (Restaurants, Shopping, Activities, etc...)

_____

_____

_____

Guest Names: _____

Dates Of Stay: _____ to _____

Traveling From: _____

Message To Host:

Favorite Lasting Memories From My Stay: _____

_____

_____

_____

Places I recommend To Others: (Restaurants, Shopping, Activities, etc...)

_____

_____

_____

Guest Names: _____

Dates Of Stay: _____ to _____

Traveling From: _____

Message To Host:

Favorite Lasting Memories From My Stay: _____

_____

_____

_____

Places I recommend To Others: (Restaurants, Shopping, Activities, etc...)

_____

_____

_____

Guest Names: _____

Message To Host:

Dates Of Stay: _____ to _____

Traveling From: _____

Favorite Lasting Memories From My Stay: _____

_____

_____

_____

Places I recommend To Others: (Restaurants, Shopping, Activities, etc...)

_____

_____

_____

Guest Names: _____

Dates Of Stay: _____ to _____

Traveling From: _____

Message To Host:

Favorite Lasting Memories From My Stay: _____

_____

_____

_____

Places I recommend To Others: (Restaurants, Shopping, Activities, etc...)

_____

_____

_____

Guest Names: _____

Dates Of Stay: _____ to _____

Traveling From: _____

Message To Host:

Favorite Lasting Memories From My Stay: _____

_____

_____

_____

Places I recommend To Others: (Restaurants, Shopping, Activities, etc...)

_____

_____

_____

Guest Names: _____

Dates Of Stay: _____ to _____

Traveling From: _____

Message To Host:

Favorite Lasting Memories From My Stay: _____

_____

_____

_____

Places I recommend To Others: (Restaurants, Shopping, Activities, etc...)

_____

_____

_____

Guest Names: _____

Dates Of Stay: _____ to _____

Traveling From: _____

Message To Host:

Favorite Lasting Memories From My Stay: _____

_____

_____

_____

Places I recommend To Others: (Restaurants, Shopping, Activities, etc...)

_____

_____

_____

Guest Names: _____

Dates Of Stay: _____ to _____

Traveling From: _____

Message To Host:

Favorite Lasting Memories From My Stay: _____

_____

_____

_____

Places I recommend To Others: (Restaurants, Shopping, Activities, etc...)

_____

_____

_____

Guest Names: _____

Dates Of Stay: _____ to _____

Traveling From: _____

Message To Host:

Favorite Lasting Memories From My Stay: _____

_____

_____

_____

Places I recommend To Others: (Restaurants, Shopping, Activities, etc...)

_____

_____

_____

Guest Names: _____

Dates Of Stay: _____ to _____

Traveling From: _____

Message To Host:

Favorite Lasting Memories From My Stay: _____

_____

_____

_____

Places I recommend To Others: (Restaurants, Shopping, Activities, etc...)

_____

_____

_____

Guest Names: _____

Dates Of Stay: _____ to _____

Traveling From: _____

Message To Host:

Favorite Lasting Memories From My Stay: _____

_____

_____

_____

Places I recommend To Others: (Restaurants, Shopping, Activities, etc...)

_____

_____

_____

Guest Names: _____

Dates Of Stay: _____ to _____

Traveling From: _____

Message To Host:

Favorite Lasting Memories From My Stay: _____

_____

_____

_____

Places I recommend To Others: (Restaurants, Shopping, Activities, etc...)

_____

_____

_____

Guest Names: _____

Dates Of Stay: _____ to _____

Traveling From: _____

Message To Host:

Favorite Lasting Memories From My Stay: _____

_____

_____

_____

Places I recommend To Others: (Restaurants, Shopping, Activities, etc...)

_____

_____

_____

Guest Names: _____

Dates Of Stay: _____ to _____

Traveling From: _____

Message To Host:

Favorite Lasting Memories From My Stay: _____

_____

_____

_____

Places I recommend To Others: (Restaurants, Shopping, Activities, etc...)

_____

_____

_____

Guest Names: _____

Dates Of Stay: _____ to _____

Traveling From: _____

Message To Host:

Favorite Lasting Memories From My Stay: _____

_____

_____

_____

Places I recommend To Others: (Restaurants, Shopping, Activities, etc...)

_____

_____

_____

Guest Names: _____

Dates Of Stay: _____ to _____

Traveling From: _____

Message To Host:

Favorite Lasting Memories From My Stay: _____

_____

_____

_____

Places I recommend To Others: (Restaurants, Shopping, Activities, etc...)

_____

_____

_____

Guest Names: _____

Dates Of Stay: _____ to _____

Traveling From: _____

Message To Host:

Favorite Lasting Memories From My Stay: _____

_____

_____

_____

Places I recommend To Others: (Restaurants, Shopping, Activities, etc...)

_____

_____

_____

Guest Names: _____

Dates Of Stay: _____ to _____

Traveling From: _____

Message To Host:

Favorite Lasting Memories From My Stay: _____

_____

_____

_____

Places I recommend To Others: (Restaurants, Shopping, Activities, etc...)

_____

_____

_____

Guest Names: _____

Dates Of Stay: _____ to _____

Traveling From: _____

Message To Host:

Favorite Lasting Memories From My Stay: _____

_____

_____

_____

Places I recommend To Others: (Restaurants, Shopping, Activities, etc...)

_____

_____

_____

Guest Names: _____

Dates Of Stay: _____ to _____

Traveling From: _____

Message To Host:

Favorite Lasting Memories From My Stay: _____

_____

_____

_____

Places I recommend To Others: (Restaurants, Shopping, Activities, etc...)

_____

_____

_____

Guest Names: _____

Dates Of Stay: _____ to _____

Traveling From: _____

Message To Host:

Favorite Lasting Memories From My Stay: _____

_____

_____

_____

Places I recommend To Others: (Restaurants, Shopping, Activities, etc...)

_____

_____

_____

Guest Names: _____

Message To Host:

Dates Of Stay: _____ to _____

Traveling From: _____

Favorite Lasting Memories From My Stay: _____

_____

_____

_____

Places I recommend To Others: (Restaurants, Shopping, Activities, etc...)

_____

_____

_____

Guest Names: _____

Dates Of Stay: _____ to _____

Traveling From: _____

Message To Host:

Favorite Lasting Memories From My Stay: _____

_____

_____

_____

Places I recommend To Others: (Restaurants, Shopping, Activities, etc...)

_____

_____

_____

Guest Names: _____

Dates Of Stay: _____ to _____

Traveling From: _____

Message To Host:

Favorite Lasting Memories From My Stay: _____

_____

_____

_____

Places I recommend To Others: (Restaurants, Shopping, Activities, etc...)

_____

_____

_____

Guest Names: _____

Dates Of Stay: _____ to _____

Traveling From: _____

Message To Host:

Favorite Lasting Memories From My Stay: _____

_____

_____

_____

Places I recommend To Others: (Restaurants, Shopping, Activities, etc...)

_____

_____

_____

Guest Names: _____

Dates Of Stay: _____ to _____

Traveling From: _____

Message To Host:

Favorite Lasting Memories From My Stay: _____

_____

_____

_____

Places I recommend To Others: (Restaurants, Shopping, Activities, etc...)

_____

_____

_____

Guest Names: _____

Dates Of Stay: _____ to _____

Traveling From: _____

Message To Host:

Favorite Lasting Memories From My Stay: _____

_____

_____

_____

Places I recommend To Others: (Restaurants, Shopping, Activities, etc...)

_____

_____

_____

Guest Names: _____

Dates Of Stay: _____ to _____

Traveling From: _____

Message To Host:

Favorite Lasting Memories From My Stay: _____

_____

_____

_____

Places I recommend To Others: (Restaurants, Shopping, Activities, etc...)

_____

_____

_____

Guest Names: _____

Dates Of Stay: _____ to _____

Traveling From: _____

Favorite Lasting Memories From My Stay: _____

_____

_____

_____

Places I recommend To Others: (Restaurants, Shopping, Activities, etc...)

_____

_____

_____

Message To Host:

Guest Names: _____

Dates Of Stay: _____ to _____

Traveling From: _____

Message To Host:

Favorite Lasting Memories From My Stay: _____

_____

_____

_____

Places I recommend To Others: (Restaurants, Shopping, Activities, etc...)

_____

_____

_____

Guest Names: _____

Dates Of Stay: _____ to _____

Traveling From: _____

Message To Host:

Favorite Lasting Memories From My Stay: _____

_____

_____

_____

Places I recommend To Others: (Restaurants, Shopping, Activities, etc...)

_____

_____

_____

Guest Names: _____

Dates Of Stay: _____ to _____

Traveling From: _____

Message To Host:

Favorite Lasting Memories From My Stay: _____

_____

_____

_____

Places I recommend To Others: (Restaurants, Shopping, Activities, etc...)

_____

_____

_____

Guest Names: _____

Dates Of Stay: _____ to _____

Traveling From: _____

Message To Host:

Favorite Lasting Memories From My Stay: _____

_____

_____

_____

Places I recommend To Others: (Restaurants, Shopping, Activities, etc...)

_____

_____

_____

Guest Names: _____

Dates Of Stay: _____ to _____

Traveling From: _____

Message To Host:

Favorite Lasting Memories From My Stay: _____

_____

_____

_____

Places I recommend To Others: (Restaurants, Shopping, Activities, etc...)

_____

_____

_____

Guest Names: _____

Dates Of Stay: _____ to _____

Traveling From: _____

Message To Host:

Favorite Lasting Memories From My Stay: _____

_____

_____

_____

Places I recommend To Others: (Restaurants, Shopping, Activities, etc...)

_____

_____

_____

Guest Names: _____

Dates Of Stay: _____ to _____

Traveling From: _____

Message To Host:

Favorite Lasting Memories From My Stay: _____

_____

_____

_____

Places I recommend To Others: (Restaurants, Shopping, Activities, etc...)

_____

_____

_____

Guest Names: _____

Dates Of Stay: _____ to _____

Traveling From: _____

Message To Host:

Favorite Lasting Memories From My Stay: _____

_____

_____

_____

Places I recommend To Others: (Restaurants, Shopping, Activities, etc...)

_____

_____

_____

Guest Names: _____

Dates Of Stay: _____ to _____

Traveling From: _____

Message To Host:

Favorite Lasting Memories From My Stay: _____

_____

_____

_____

Places I recommend To Others: (Restaurants, Shopping, Activities, etc...)

_____

_____

_____

Guest Names: _____

Dates Of Stay: _____ to _____

Traveling From: _____

Message To Host:

Favorite Lasting Memories From My Stay: _____

_____

_____

_____

Places I recommend To Others: (Restaurants, Shopping, Activities, etc...)

_____

_____

_____

Guest Names: _____

Dates Of Stay: _____ to _____

Traveling From: _____

Message To Host:

Favorite Lasting Memories From My Stay: _____

_____

_____

_____

Places I recommend To Others: (Restaurants, Shopping, Activities, etc...)

_____

_____

_____

Guest Names: _____

Dates Of Stay: _____ to _____

Traveling From: _____

Message To Host:

Favorite Lasting Memories From My Stay: _____

_____

_____

_____

Places I recommend To Others: (Restaurants, Shopping, Activities, etc...)

_____

_____

_____

Guest Names: _____

Dates Of Stay: _____ to _____

Traveling From: _____

Message To Host:

Favorite Lasting Memories From My Stay: _____

_____

_____

_____

Places I recommend To Others: (Restaurants, Shopping, Activities, etc...)

_____

_____

_____

Guest Names: _____

Dates Of Stay: _____ to _____

Traveling From: _____

Message To Host:

Favorite Lasting Memories From My Stay: _____

_____

_____

_____

Places I recommend To Others: (Restaurants, Shopping, Activities, etc...)

_____

_____

_____

Guest Names: _____

Dates Of Stay: _____ to _____

Message To Host:

Traveling From: _____

Favorite Lasting Memories From My Stay: _____

_____

_____

_____

Places I recommend To Others: (Restaurants, Shopping, Activities, etc...)

_____

_____

_____

Guest Names: _____

Dates Of Stay: _____ to _____

Traveling From: _____

Message To Host:

Favorite Lasting Memories From My Stay: _____

_____

_____

_____

Places I recommend To Others: (Restaurants, Shopping, Activities, etc...)

_____

_____

_____

Guest Names: _____

Dates Of Stay: _____ to _____

Traveling From: _____

Message To Host:

Favorite Lasting Memories From My Stay: _____

_____

_____

_____

Places I recommend To Others: (Restaurants, Shopping, Activities, etc...)

_____

_____

_____

Guest Names: _____

Dates Of Stay: _____ to _____

Traveling From: _____

Message To Host:

Favorite Lasting Memories From My Stay: _____

_____

_____

_____

Places I recommend To Others: (Restaurants, Shopping, Activities, etc...)

_____

_____

_____

Guest Names: _____

Dates Of Stay: _____ to _____

Traveling From: _____

Message To Host:

Favorite Lasting Memories From My Stay: _____

_____

_____

_____

Places I recommend To Others: (Restaurants, Shopping, Activities, etc...)

_____

_____

_____

Guest Names: _____

Dates Of Stay: _____ to _____

Traveling From: _____

Message To Host:

Favorite Lasting Memories From My Stay: _____

_____

_____

_____

Places I recommend To Others: (Restaurants, Shopping, Activities, etc...)

_____

_____

_____

Guest Names: _____

Dates Of Stay: _____ to _____

Traveling From: _____

Message To Host:

Favorite Lasting Memories From My Stay: _____

_____

_____

_____

Places I recommend To Others: (Restaurants, Shopping, Activities, etc...)

_____

_____

_____

Guest Names: _____

Dates Of Stay: _____ to _____

Traveling From: _____

Message To Host:

Favorite Lasting Memories From My Stay: _____

_____

_____

_____

Places I recommend To Others: (Restaurants, Shopping, Activities, etc...)

_____

_____

_____

Guest Names: _____

Message To Host:

Dates Of Stay: _____ to _____

Traveling From: _____

Favorite Lasting Memories From My Stay: _____

_____

_____

_____

Places I recommend To Others: (Restaurants, Shopping, Activities, etc...)

_____

_____

_____

Guest Names: _____

Dates Of Stay: _____ to _____

Traveling From: _____

Message To Host:

Favorite Lasting Memories From My Stay: _____

_____

_____

_____

Places I recommend To Others: (Restaurants, Shopping, Activities, etc...)

_____

_____

_____

Guest Names: _____

Dates Of Stay: _____ to _____

Traveling From: _____

Message To Host:

Favorite Lasting Memories From My Stay: _____

_____

_____

_____

Places I recommend To Others: (Restaurants, Shopping, Activities, etc...)

_____

_____

_____

Guest Names: _____

Dates Of Stay: _____ to _____

Traveling From: _____

Message To Host:

Favorite Lasting Memories From My Stay: _____

_____

_____

_____

Places I recommend To Others: (Restaurants, Shopping, Activities, etc...)

_____

_____

_____

Guest Names: _____

Dates Of Stay: _____ to _____

Traveling From: _____

Message To Host:

Favorite Lasting Memories From My Stay: _____

_____

_____

_____

Places I recommend To Others: (Restaurants, Shopping, Activities, etc...)

_____

_____

_____

Guest Names: _____

Dates Of Stay: _____ to _____

Traveling From: _____

Message To Host:

Favorite Lasting Memories From My Stay: _____

_____

_____

_____

Places I recommend To Others: (Restaurants, Shopping, Activities, etc...)

_____

_____

_____

Guest Names: _____

Message To Host:

Dates Of Stay: _____ to _____

Traveling From: _____

Favorite Lasting Memories From My Stay: _____

_____

_____

_____

Places I recommend To Others: (Restaurants, Shopping, Activities, etc...)

_____

_____

_____

Guest Names: _____

Dates Of Stay: _____ to _____

Traveling From: _____

Message To Host:

Favorite Lasting Memories From My Stay: _____

_____

_____

_____

Places I recommend To Others: (Restaurants, Shopping, Activities, etc...)

_____

_____

_____

Guest Names: _____

Dates Of Stay: _____ to _____

Traveling From: _____

Message To Host:

Favorite Lasting Memories From My Stay: _____

_____

_____

_____

Places I recommend To Others: (Restaurants, Shopping, Activities, etc...)

_____

_____

_____

Guest Names: _____

Dates Of Stay: _____ to _____

Traveling From: _____

Favorite Lasting Memories From My Stay: _____

Message To Host:

_____

_____

_____

Places I recommend To Others: (Restaurants, Shopping, Activities, etc...)

_____

_____

_____

Guest Names: _____

Dates Of Stay: _____ to _____

Traveling From: _____

Message To Host:

Favorite Lasting Memories From My Stay: _____

_____

_____

_____

Places I recommend To Others: (Restaurants, Shopping, Activities, etc...)

_____

_____

_____

Made in the USA
Monee, IL
11 May 2023

33484098R00068